LUCY'S MINI MOJO MANUAL

A Short Guide to Sassy Self-Evolution

by **Lucy Baker**

*In my book, I've incorporated
the pronoun 'they' where possible,
rather than 'she' or 'he' to encompass
and support All in their journey to Self.*

Contents

Preface

That breath you just took ...could be your last.
I know you don't notice it.
I know you've gotten complacent.
I know you think you've got lots of time.

All you have is Now.

Wouldn't it be handy for us to know exactly when we're going to die? *Sure*, it's utterly petrifying to have that Death Clock counting down — but honestly, if you're anything like me, you need a deadline to get anything done.

My job is to kick your ass into realising that if you don't follow your intuition, heart and purpose - and love as much as you can while your heart's still beating, then you may miss the opportunity to do so.

I've been working with Spirit for 51 years. And I know that the biggest regret of dead people is the amount of love they did *not* freely give and did not generously open to receive.

I say *'generously'*, because it's a gift to allow others to be of service to you. Just going to others won't work. There must be an *equal exchange of energy* for all of us to come into balance and influence the level of healing that the world needs.

Mojo is the best remedy I know that will take you out of the seriousness and pain of your life and into the vibrancy you need to embrace intuition, happiness, self-worth and a sense of abundance. It's what I focus on in **The Lucy Daily**, my free service to the world, via daily social media posts that I've written (yes, every day, give or take a few long-haul flights) for almost 7 years.

The definition of *'Mojo'* can be described as *'influencing with magical powers'* as if you are casting yourself in your own spell. For me, it is a deliberate climb out of the pit of low energy thoughts into the space where birds fly. When we take ourselves lightly, we see different perspectives and have more chance of connecting with loved ones in Spirit, our guides and our own innate wisdom.

You're more ready to create a new chapter for yourself than your thoughts think.

Have you noticed any hints from the universe about your readiness?

When we've still sitting in front of a lesson that's expired, situations get super intense and difficult. Emotionally, you'll feel restless, unseen, frightened, angry or sodden with grief at how your life is looking.

These are all signs that you're preparing to write a new story.

To choose who you now want to be.

To put you first, for a change.

To stop living your life through the experiences of other people and to claim your ownership of You.

There's a reason you are still alive — despite everything!

We're going to boost your Mojo, raise your vibrations. You'll discover how to take yourself lightly and your purpose seriously — not the other way around.

Stuck humans believe change is difficult. Simplicity is the real discipline. Just like my favourite Australian sulphur-crested cockatoo who soars across the sky above my house gleefully, loudly, visible in all its glory, you don't need a university degree to empower yourself.

You're the conductor of the orchestra, the driver of your car – and if you follow the advice in this Manual, you'll go on to inspire countless others simply by you *being yourself* rather than doing anything for them. *Less effort, more reward* will become your new mantra.

You'll learn how to put your mind in its place so that it stops running your life.

You'll understand how to make your *inner knowing* louder than your mental knowledge.

You'll develop a self-appreciation and gratitude for yourself, and you won't feel the need for all that external approval you've been dependent on to identify your gorgeousness.

Synchronicity rules your life, whether you've realised it or not.

You weren't just *randomly dropped* onto this planet at this time. There's an order to all of this underneath the mayhem. If chaos and coincidence were in charge, you'd see people suddenly dying in strange places. Cars veering off peaceful roads as hearts suddenly stopped, shoppers dropping dead in aisle three of the local supermarket. We make choices all the time with our energy. We just don't realise it because it's unconscious.

Who you think you are is just a fraction of who you *really* are.

We need your light.

It's high time you became the author of your own Destiny.

Chapter 1
stop right now

When you woke up today, you had many of the same thoughts you had yesterday. Your order of the morning followed the same ritual, your body language and conversational style was the same, as was your amount of eye contact and range of feelings.

There is a certain safety to structure. However, when structure starts to restrict our development, *it becomes a prison.*

Think about your school years and what you feel was of great value. It was probably more to do with the life skills, the emotional experiences, the friendships than geometry or frog dissection.

My sister, an ordained Buddhist nun, was instrumental in setting up the first Kadampa Buddhist school in Britain a decade or so ago — so progress is happening in our classrooms. Imagine how your life might have looked had you learned all about compassion, empathy, clear communication, healthy boundaries and anger management in primary school.

Beyond our schools, almost every modern society rewards academic and intellectual success at the cost of the arts, creativity and intuitive leadership. Head over heart, every time — bizarre when you consider that it is the heart that physically maintains human life rather than the brain.

Now, it's what you do with your brain that'll either render you stagnant or keep you progressing.

Here's a question for you: *what is the dominant vibration within the thoughts that you repeatedly think from day to day?* Are your thoughts more fearful than appreciative? Do you worry more than you trust? Do you doubt more than hope?

The good news is, how you think, is just a habit. The bad news is how you think is just a habit. Your mind is like an old floppy disk — yes, one of those — that always goes back to what it knows. I could describe it as a USB, but that would be way too modern to hold the generations of repetitive clan rules that have saturated your very being over all these years of your life, so I'll stick to the 1980s technology!

1. *The original You was perfect.*

All babies are born with a sense of *unconscious perfection.* Then, for most of us, we develop a sense of *conscious imperfection* derived from the conditions of childhood and adolescence. Spiritually, babies remember where they come from. This sense of connection, despite the new experience of being in a separate individual human body, allows for a calming energy that we feel when we hold them. If you knew where your real home was, you'd probably feel safer and more connected, too.

Your task is to become *consciously perfect* –to understand that you're lovable just by being who you are, that there is nothing innately wrong with you, that every single person on the planet is *a little crazy in their own special way* and that you can continue to grow yourself once you accept who you are, in all your light and all your shadow.

2. *You've been conditioned to love conditionally*

When we go into drama, all we're doing is cranking up
the old computer, blowing off the dust and inserting
the floppy disk again. Your mindset, in its current state,
is here to remind you of the past and the consequences
of breaking the rules of the clan that you're supposed
to adhere to, if you want to be loved. To fall in love
with yourself in an unconditional way, you will have to
chuck out the 1980s technology. Sometimes, you may
need to leave the clan to find yourself. Some return,
others find another tribe who love them for who they
are.

'Unconditional love' is the giving or receiving of love
without the expectation that it will be returned. Most people
have no idea about how to love in this way, because
they have only experienced this in the early stages of
life, as a baby. For others, conditional love happened
as early as being in the womb — which means, energetically, upon birth a clear life script would already be
present: *'I am unworthy of love as I am.'*

3. *It's never too late to become a rebel with a cause*

Whenever you break a rule, discomfort follows. Practice getting comfortable with being uncomfortable in small baby steps, for example taking a different route to work or striking up a conversation with a stranger that feels intuitively safe. The more you try out different ways of being, the more you'll relax into it when you realise the sky is not going to fall down on you.

Politics will show you how dictators, past and present have utilised the tools of submission, obedience, dependence on outside approval to control the people. Once you realise there are no chosen few and that everyone faces the same themes of loss, shame, rage and self-approval as you are, you step out of the story. Like Nelson Mandela or the Dalai Lama, you have both light and shadow. History will show them as two men who got stuck in their own egos at times and made their own fair share of mistakes. Own your equality.

4. *There is nothing sacred about tradition unless it works*

Consider yourself the spiritual leader in your family. What new rituals, rules or systems would you like to create that builds confidence in your loved ones? One of my favourite things to do when my family gathers around the table is to combine dessert with appreciation. As the evening draws to a gentle close, I'll encourage everyone to look around the table and notice who they're with. Then, as the smiles appear on faces, each will look to the person on the left of them and speak an appreciation. The receiver can then *practice receiving* by simply saying "thank you" before turning to the person on his or her left, and so on.

Your soul's task is to not merely repeat the patterns of your mother or father, but to exceed his or her limitations. Just as the next generation would hope to exceed yours. Right now, *stop* … and notice what you're proud of about who you are, in this moment. In what way have you been a more loving or more present parent than the one you had? And if you are not a parent, ask yourself, *'in what way have I been a more loving adult?'* Sometimes it's only when we look back, that we realise how far we've come.

Chapter 2
are you present?

Between the ages of four and nine, I lived with my father and the nanny he married within six weeks of hiring her to take care of us. Life was stressful, the mood was volatile, and I was usually the scapegoat for any trouble that went down.

I became a highly anxious child and was always travel-sick. Family trips were usually experienced lying down in the back of the car. I would have a limited view of the passing scenery, but the tops of the trees I could see against the grey sky, would give me a sense of peace that was the opposite of the tension in the car.

As adults we may easily drive our own car, but we're not so adept at thinking independently. Our need for outside approval will result in us staying in bad situations long after we should have left and allowing our personal freedom to be influenced by the demands of others who need our energies.

Sometimes the part of us that's driving our car, is our inner child – you know, the one that holds all the emotions that we haven't yet resolved. The part of us that really wants other people to love us – and love ourselves.

Usually this has come from learning that *your worth is dependent on what you give to others rather than what you give yourself.* Of course, this is especially true if you have been born female, as culturally and energetically, we are raised mostly to be good, to be quiet, to express sadness rather than anger, to reduce our light so that we can fit in with others and to never put ourselves first for fear of being labelled 'selfish'. We've become used to listening to authority figures outside of ourselves who tell us what to do, how to dress, what believe in and how we should treat ourselves.

To keep ourselves safe, we stay obedient and small. To maintain this invisibility, we will often project fear and worry from the past into the future, almost like a warning. With a few exceptions, most women, at home or in career, have been labelled 'difficult' because they've desired autonomy. Consequences make us lose our breath and ourselves. In our busy lives, it takes discipline to just breathe and stay resolutely in the moment of Now. But, when we do, we enter Power.

1. *Stay here now and take a breath*

The present moment is a neutral place. For me, it's like standing in the middle of a meadow of sunflowers. It feels calm and unadulterated by thought. Through repetition of habit, it's easy to begin to hear *three sounds* around you, perhaps the singing of a bird in a tree, the sound of a breeze or the distant hum of lawnmower. You can use these as an entry into deeper relaxation.

And, as you breathe into the present moment, become aware of the calmness in your belly, the headquarters of your intuition. Your task is to, moment by moment, *extend the time you stay in the present.* Repetition builds strength — and for you to manifest what you truly want rather than what you don't, becoming comfortable with being in the present is where the power lies.

2. *What you think so you create*

As soon as you climb back into your head with its flashing red lights and frantic conveyor belt of urgent thoughts, addictive worries and dramatic fears, you have left the peaceful neutral zone of Presence and have returned to the battlefield. Now, choose which direction you want to go in — towards the fighting or away from it. Naturally, you want peace. Who doesn't? In practice however, you may be hard-wired for war, like any soldier in survival mode, on alert, belly tight and head reactive.

As you think, so your feelings will mirror these thoughts. Your feelings will inform your energy and your ability to manifest … and inevitably you will attract the situation that you have been repetitively thinking about. So, test this out! Think of a time that you've worked yourself up into such a state of worry or anxiety, that you've started to feel physical effects. To change direction, do what shamans do. Breathe, ground yourself and listen to a calmer rhythm of a repetitive sound, like a drum. You are the magnet.

3. Stop stopping yourself from being present

Just like an awkward silence on a first date, you may be uncomfortable with the gaps between doing and thinking. You may rush to fill the empty spaces which, in turn, will prevent you from receiving any new information or possibilities. If busyness is a status symbol of success these days, notice whether you respond to feeling uncomfortable or uncertain by immediately getting busy.

Choose a day in the next month in which you can practice *doing less and being more*. This can be a challenge if you use to constantly being on the move. It is important therefore to remember that if this was your last day on earth you might want to spend it by just being with people that you love. Not doing a whole lot except holding each other and enjoying each other's company. As you get used to being in this precious present one day at a time, so you can incorporate more beingness into every day.

4. *Abrupt events shatter belief systems*

A belief is simply a thought you keep thinking over and over again. In time, this pattern of thinking will become your truth. However, if your soul is unhappy with the status quo and wants you to grow beyond a certain belief, inevitably your life will create a situation in which you'll be forced to experience another perspective. When shocking events occur, we are taken out of our comfort zones of complacency and woken up.

One of my clients was a workaholic. His whole life was his job as a travelling salesman building up his frequent flyer miles and spending more time in airports than he did at home with his wife and sons. He had high blood pressure and had a charming but stubborn personality. One morning, on his way to the airport he suffered an aneurysm which resulted in him lying flat on a hospital bed for months in recovery, during which time he learned how to surrender to being in the moment. His biggest regret? That he overruled his intuition and his family's desires in favour of a job that didn't care as much about him as he did about external approval. Last time he contacted me, he was happily retired, focusing on his new hobby of joy and reconnecting to his family. In every cloud, there is a silver lining.

Chapter 3
are you a Ferrari?

Everyone likes a good car. One of your ultimate aims might to buy your very own dream car, with its shiny beautiful exterior and its glossy smooth interior, motor purring, speedy and efficient – and with heads turning in awe as you drive down the road.

For right now, as long as it has four wheels, a heater for winter and a music system that works, you might feel you have everything you need. If it gets you from A to B, it's enough, right?

Imagine your car – the luxury car you always wanted. Perhaps a convertible, or perhaps a Ferrari. It's easy to picture a Ferrari. It has a pretty exterior but what if it's a Fiat Panda underneath? What if it just looks good because it gains approval?

A lot of people drive the cars they want to feel like, just like they wear the clothes they want to fit into a certain group, class or community with. When I was 22, I lived in Germany for three months, in a small town called Kaiserslautern. I wanted to meet people my age, I wanted to learn the language and I wanted to fit in. So, what I did when I got off the train from England, was go to the nearest charity clothes shop, donate the ones I had worn in London and swap them for the baggy trousers, T-shirt and long coat I had seen on the young people in the streets.

I remember the feeling of relief when I exited the shop. At least I looked like everyone else now. Soon, I realised it wouldn't be that easy – I'd have to learn the language so well that other people knew exactly what I was trying to say. I'd have to get a job and make some money in order to afford to live in my little attic room. I'd also have to contribute confidently to conversations reverberating among the pub circles of aware youth discussing everything from racism to personal evolution.

It was clear. My greatest challenge would be transforming my Fiat into a car with substance.

My partner informs me the ideal car is actually a Porsche Macan S, because it has all the performance of a sports car and the practicality of a 4WD which allows it to cover all terrains.

1. *Your outside is not as important as your inside*

You know within seven seconds of meeting someone, whether you like them or not. Everything is about energy. Sometimes, we have developed the habit of trusting someone's words, rather than how we feel about their vibes. We take things at face value – which leads us immediately into trouble.

By working on your inner self, you can become so authentic that you exude your own special charisma. Instinctively, humans – like every animal in nature – *know what truth feels like*. The more you shrug off the urge to look the opposite of your low self-esteem or insecurity, the more time you'll have to focus on clearing out the reasons why you first began to feel like that.

2. There is a precious jewel inside you

Someone once asked the sculptor, Michelangelo, how he was able to carve his exquisite human figures out of large blocks of marble. In response, the artist said that he was simply looking for the perfectly formed figure already sculpted and hidden inside. They say that if God wanted to hide, they would hide inside the body of a human being, because it's the last place we'd look.

You are denying your own fabulousness. The person you are becoming through your developing sense of awareness, is similar to the marble being transformed. If you can practice accepting that, in spite of every-thing you ever heard, you have within you a remarkable, beautiful authentic self just waiting for you to open the doors to it, feel it and let it grow stronger than any doubt, any distrust, any self-criticism – imagine how you would feel.

Even though you don't notice it as much as you will in the future, there is an excited inner Michelangelo inside you just itching to get on with the job of being the artist of your destiny.

3. Procrastination doesn't get a free ride

When you are preparing to travel towards authenticity, you'll need to not only remove as much excess baggage that you're aware of, but also that inner procrastinator. Before you know it, they'll slip into the back seat, murmuring that you still need them as part of your timing and, besides, they've always been with you ever since you started losing yourself – so you're old friends, right? Wrong! It's never been your ally. It's been responsible for missed opportunities. There are doors that open for only for a few moments in time, that your intuition urges you to walk through. Even though you may not be able to see the full picture of what lies beyond, your true self trusts the fact that the door is open. Procrastination comes from the old mind, and it means that you are not trusting – not trusting your instincts, but most of all, not trusting that you are always in the right place at the right time.

For this trip to be successful, you will need to have your wits about you. You will need your instincts, balanced with your logical, yet open mindset – and most of all you need faith. Faith is not a religious concept: it's a spiritual one and it means that you're listening to your soul.

4. *Even when things look bad, you're still in the Flow*

It's easy to trust your life when life flows smoothly. However, the real test is about how much you believe in the synchronicity of energy. We can say we're spiritual. We can say that we're aware and progressive. Yet, even the most spiritual, aware person can drop the idea of trusting in the flow when things take a turn for the worse. We have suddenly gone from trusting in the universe to being fickle.

Commitment is understanding that you're always in the flow, whether or not your inner control freak demands a guarantee of eternal happiness. Sometimes we learn the most from the horrible events and situations in life. Imagine the flow is like a river that never stops. If you hang onto an overhanging tree branch, the river will still keep flowing. It'll just be you that is being left behind. If that's you right now, drop back into the river and trust that your soul's journey is taking you somewhere. Timing is everything.

Chapter 4
the state of your engine

When you were a child, you were gifted with a natural sense of self-acceptance. It wasn't ego seeking approval, it wasn't a mask concealing deeper feelings, it wasn't arrogance believing you were better than someone else on the planet. It was a natural sense of your own loveability.

Then someone – usually a parent, guardian or a teacher – came along and changed that, with their words of disapproval, with their rules of what emotions could be acknowledged, what emotions were not allowed and with their facial expressions and tones of voice. You were told that you were naughty, bad, misbehaved or just plain wrong about your idea that you were, in essence, love itself.

Now is time to reclaim the real you, to develop the habit of self-acceptance that'll open you up once again to new opportunities, strengthen your belief in yourself and a certainty of confidence that you can do anything you choose and become the person you're destined to be.

In my childhood, I was continually shown and told that I was a difficult child, that I was so unlovable that I was removed from my family. Once I was in a safer place, it was only through the love and care of a healthy parent that I was able to begin to believe in myself again and know that I was blessed.

One of the ways I began to let love into my heart again, was to appreciate myself. So how well do you appreciate yourself? How many thoughts of self-love have to compete with self- criticism, on a daily basis?

If I had to ask you to give me two minutes of sharing everything you love about who you are, rather than what you do – would you fill that time easily, almost without thinking? Alternatively, if I asked you to give me two minutes of sharing everything about yourself that you dislike, doubt or criticise, would those two minutes be filled up and spill over into five, 10 or even 20 minutes? If it's hard for you to find self-appreciation, start this new habit. What you focus on, grows.

1. Remember who you used to be

Find a photograph of you as a little child. Take it out from storage and place it somewhere where you will see it every day. Look at that little face looking back at you. This child is still there, deep inside of you, and they're the one who needs the love you keep giving to other people first. They're the one who needs to be heard, to be accepted, to be adored and to become your most important priority.

The first step of your return to power, of your personal growth and healing, is to tune in to the smallest part of you. To make new rules which allow them, perhaps for the first time in their life, to feel every feeling and to be allowed to express it in ways that are safe for them and everybody else. By listening to your gut and then making time to acknowledge what's coming up emotionally, without judgement, will make you very, very powerful.

2. Become a safe place for you

You build safety inside yourself, by being available to yourself. When your little child is feeling grief or anger, it's important to make time that same day to let those feelings come up. To do this, you need to accept that emotions are only arising in order for you to notice them and then to release them, to let them out.

If you bury them down again, they'll become stuck, and they will block your progress. Think of all emotions as the weather in nature – happiness could be sunshine, fear could be wind, grief could be rain. Why would you try to hold back the weather? Your mission is to allow it to blow through you and then to let it go.

It's only emotion – it doesn't have to be attached to a story or a judgement or criticism. Now that you are an adult, you can make your own rules. The healthiest people understand that every emotion is perfectly acceptable and has its own place. From now on, when you feel it, let it rise up and leave you without your mind getting too involved.

3. *What you repress, someone else will express*

What we need in all our relationships, is a sense of safety. This is different to the definition of security most people have, which is usually financial. Real safety is about feeling free to be ourselves and to be accepted as such. In relationships with other people, safety is knowing that they are trustworthy, able to give and receive communication and steadfast in their love and acceptance of us. We won't find this in other people, unless we feel safe within ourselves. We won't fully trust anyone else, unless we trust our own intuition. If we're not feeling safe within ourselves, our inner child won't feel safe enough to express everything they needs, to finally heal and release all of that pent-up emotion it's been carrying for all of these years.

If we're unsafe, we'll attract people who mirror our feelings of un-safety. They'll block off their own feelings, feel low self-worth, sabotage their own happiness with fears and doubts. And, because they're not listening to themselves, they won't be present with anyone else. If you make yourself your own self-loving life partner, you'll meet someone else who does exactly the same thing.

4. *Take your mind to obedience classes*

A new habit takes time to develop. Your brain is full of neuronal pathways, well-beaten tracks that your thoughts have been used to travelling down, day after day, moment by moment. To create a new path, you'll need to create it with an abundance of thoughts that support its flourishing. Imagine your mind is like a naughty puppy, running all over the busy highway, dodging cars and not listening to its owner. Now, you're putting a leash on your puppy and you're going to train it to think higher thoughts.

Wake up each morning and say, "thank you". Be grateful that you have another day to become who you are supposed to be. Be grateful that you can influence your loved ones and those around you in your community with sunshine, instead of gloomy clouds. People are like flowers – they need sunshine to grow, they need care and attention. And most importantly, so do you.

Chapter 5
you're in a dream team

Because the Universe has your back, it has already
planned ahead and made sure you have an amazing
team of supporters around you. The tricky thing is,
most of them are probably on the Spirit plane. Once
you start trusting in your intuition, you'll find that these
welcoming, warm energies – often in the guise of a
beloved grandmother or familiar face – will visit you as
often as they can.

The most opportune time for Spirit to connect with
you, is when the mind is in the calm present or asleep.
You may find yourself in a dream, sitting in a meadow
having a picnic with a loved one in Spirit. You might
hear words in your ear, words of wisdom that can guide
you forward or reassure you. If you learn to keep your
physical body very still as you gently wake up, you can
train yourself to remember three important aspects of
a dream you had during the night. Your daydreams and
meditations will also be opportunities for connection.
Ideally, if you clear a room inside your mind and toss
out all those old, lazy negative thoughts about yourself
and the world, you'll discover you can have easy one-to-
one conversations with a bunch of people in Spirit who
only want the best for you. What's more, they're proud
of how far you've come.

What I've learned through my five decades of working with Spirit, is that we have four or five beings with us at all times. As we grow and evolve, some leave us to prepare for reincarnation or ascend to higher levels, and new, often unfamiliar Spirit helpers will come in.

For instance, if you decided to open your creativity as a way to access joy and healing, within a few weeks you would attract a soul who used to be an art teacher in their last life. If you needed to get super-organised and prepare for a very logical path of career, you might attract a manager with an excellent sense of timing and order. If you wish to turn your focus strongly towards a spiritual path, it's not unusual to attract a former spiritual sage, often in the form of a Native American spirit, a wise monk or a powerful, nurturing medicine person.

It's up to you.

1. *Make time to tone up*

Your intuition is a muscle, one that you can easily strengthen by using it regularly. Most people have grown up relying solely on the power of the mind, when in fact a balance between intelligence and intuition is crucial. Most great leaders in history respect their intuition. Albert Einstein believed it was the most important aspect of all.

Your intuition is the headquarters of your being. Without it, it's easy to get into trouble and detour from your path. I'm sure you can think of countless times you now regret going against your intuition. In those moments, when you had to make a decision or choice, you would have felt your belly tighten, your throat restricts, arise in anxiety or a sense of urgency. These are signs that your intuition is trying to get your attention. From now on, treat your intuition as the most important of your senses. Put the mind in its proper place: after all, it's only been in your body for this life, and it always thinks it's right, so it's already still a fledgling. Your intuition is connected to the percentage of your soul which lives in your body, and that percentage is connected to your Higher Self that lives up there, beyond the earth-plane. Your Higher Self can see further than you can from way down here and has been with you through many lifetimes.

2. Pay attention to messages from Nature

In your dream team, you also have what shamans describe as totems, power animals and familiars. I believe you have up to 12 totems that live in your energy and assist you in unknown ways. You may have a wolf or a bear, who protects you. Think of a time in which you somehow escaped injury, a near-miss... a moment in which you considered yourself fortunate that things had not been worse.

If you notice a bird or animal drawing your attention as you go about your day, stop and tune in. Consider what skill this particular Nature being has. A bird may have lightness, a frog has clarity, a snake has feminine power. Then ask yourself if you need to use that particular skill in your own life.

3. *Your loved ones in spirit are nicer people now*

If you had a difficult relationship with someone who has since died, it's worth knowing that they are far nicer than they ever were when they were living in a physical body. This is because they've reconnected to their Higher Self, after death. Ideally, it's much better to connect to our higher selves through trust and meditation whilst we are in a physical body living our lives, so that we can be not only guided but become harmless, loving people who can impact the planet with goodness.

However, some people are just here on earth to live on a very physical level and to not have any interest in developing spiritually. They are here to live in a state of reaction and may never seek therapy or healing, but will instead remain rigidly stuck in resentment, judgement and self-loathing. Their lives will be about service, just as yours is – but their service will be connected to harsh teachings. It's quite common for a soul to choose to be born within the family of rigid, conservative, resentful or narcissistic people, in order to learn how *not* to be that way. These souls often *volunteer* to take on the baddie roles so that you could learn the difference between darkness and light. Once they return to Spirit, they celebrate as they also reconnect to who they really are.

33

4. *You are always in a group hug*

There have been times in your life when you have felt very alone. It happens to all of us. You may have had the urge to just leave, to quit your life – yet for some reason, you decided to stay on and push through. For this, thank the invisible intervention of your soul, for it knows what's just around the corner how much happier your new chapter will be, compared to where you've been before. It's also good to thank your team of guides and helpers, for in the worst of moments and darkest of times, when you have felt completely lost, regardless as to whether you were even aware of it, they were with you. They still are. You are never alone. You have never been.

What became lost, was your connection between yourself and you. The more you love yourself, the more your heart opens, the stronger your intuition develops and you're more aware that you're continuously held in the centre of an extraordinarily loving group hug.

Chapter 6
drop the drama

There's nothing scarier than an angry woman. Not just an angry woman, but one who has settled into a stone-cold rage, with her lowered tone and steady glare like a jet-black puma you've suddenly met in the jungle one night who knows you're dinner.

Now, this may sound a bit hippyish and weird, but I'm also in the business of clearing heavy, forcefully dark energy from homes. This sort of work goes beyond a smudging of Sage and a prayer – I'm talking about knives coming through ceilings, gravel being thrown and bookcases, previously nailed to walls being flung from one end of a room to the other. In a word, poltergeist activity.

And do you know the first question I will pose to the occupants when I enter such a place? I'll ask whether there is a teenage girl having her period. Menstruation brings up a whole lot of emotion, and then a whole lot more. And teenage girls have a lot of fierce anger.

The real reason menstruating women were separated from their tribes, was not really because they were considered 'unclean'. It was because their power for energy at Moon time was magnificently, monstrously, marvellously made for manifesting. It would disrupt the energy of the group and frankly, the male leaders had no idea how to work with it.

The flipside of anger is passion. A female in full power is a force to be reckoned with. Call it menstruation a blessing from now on, not a curse. If you use your magic well and harmlessly, with awesome intent, you can do wonders. Your dreams will be deeper, your healing powers heightened, your senses enhanced and your ability to attract to you what you most focus on, accelerated.

However, most people in the world don't really know how to dance with hormones and how to wrangle their emotions into something potent yet prosperous. Men have hormones too, which is why some of them punch holes in walls and shout a lot when they're angry. The good news is that you can use the intensity of your anger to strengthen your passion, rather than do what most people do, which is to create drama. Drama only entangles you more and will drain your spirit. Maybe it's time you retired from the pantomime.

1. Choose a new way to express your anger

Most humans have learnt how to express anger in one or more of three ways. The first most popular choice is to be loud and screechy, jump up and down like a demented toddler and project rage towards someone else, in ways that include harshness, reactivity and violence. Second choice goes to those who suck it inwards, which transmutes rage into depression. The third choice is twofold, sucking your anger back in and then leaking it out like a poisonous viper, nasty, passive-aggressive, victimlike or guilt-laden, designed to manipulate.

Instead, let your inner child express emotions. The trick is to catch anger while it's still a low-level irritation, a tightness in the belly. In that moment, give yourself an immediate timeout. Walk away. Then, ask yourself, 'if I was four years old and I felt like this, how would I express it?' Usually, it's just like that child did in the supermarket that day, lying down on the floor kicking and screaming, using their physical body to help root out the intensity, in a way that wasn't projected at the nearest person. There's something sassy and tribal about the freedom of giving your inner toddler permission to roar like a tiger, punch a cushion or kick and scream on the floor. Even more importantly, you are now clearing anger safely, without harming yourself or others.

2. If you feel sad, have a fantastic cry

Grief and anger are sandwiched together in your energy. You may find that you express one more than the other, usually because of fear that you might meet with disapproval because it wasn't shown in your family of origin. Let your inner child feel her feelings. There's no need to build a story about it or try to analyse where it came from and why you're feeling this way. Just let it out.

If it's hard for you to just let go, watch a sad movie. Make sure you have all your support props, such as a hot water bottle, teddy bear, blanket, a box of tissues… perhaps a treat or two. Turn off technology, and just let the little child be. Your body may need to curl up into a fearful position one minute, and then punch a cushion the next, as emotions are so intertwined. Humans hold grief for decades. Everyone carries sadness, no matter how they appear. So, just do it. You will feel much better afterwards and definitely lighter.

3. Only if you're an actor, be dramatic

Unless you're on an actual stage or movie set, there's no need to exaggerate your pain. Remember, what you focus on grows – and quite honestly, you'd be really annoyed with yourself if you got to the end of your life and realised that drama had blocked your progress, heart, happiness and peace. Sometimes we create drama as a way to leave a relationship, be heard or victimise ourselves. Pain is sharp, simple and requires simplicity, in order to be released. Adding the fluff and performance of drama makes it all about you, rather than your commitment to simply releasing the energy of pain. Notice if you also glamorise other people's pain.

In a worldwide survey, it was found that most people on the planet had three top fears. Coming in third, was the fear of death. Second, the fear of public speaking and first… (drum roll please) … the fear of pain. We'll do anything to avoid feeling pain. We'll anaesthetise ourselves via alcohol, drugs, work, exercise, chatter, relationships or just plain ole busyness. Basically, if you're want to get happier, redefine your definition of pain. Yes… it's painful, it hurts like hell, but if you wish to attract that awesome partner, fabulous job, and get your own power back – you will need to let it out cleanly, clearly like an inner child surgeon with a scalpel.

4. *Give your inner teenager something creative to do*

An obstacle to clearing resentment, anger or drama is an ungrounded inner adolescent. They swing from one mood to another, and is given to excess, foot-stamping and sulking. They're the one who reaches for the bottle of wine when you're feeling sad or mad; blames the world for her troubles; makes sweeping statements that harshly judge everyone and talks in absolute terms. *'I hate…', 'I'll never.', 'No-one likes me', 'no matter how many times I try…'*, etc, etc, etc.

If you let them run your life, you'll swerve repeatedly off your path into the wrong relationships, act impulsively in ways that are unhealthy, max out your credit card, sabotage your happiness by choosing choices that further demean you, believe the vulnerability is a weakness, ache for outside approval whilst looking defiant and imbibe as many substances or indulge in risky behaviour as a way of feeling power. Instead, explore their creativity. They're amazing if you give them a chance to delve deep and find their passions.

Chapter 7
check your speedometer

So, you're packing the car, you're beginning to realise what needs to be left behind, you're lightening your load and you roughly know where you're headed. On your car's dashboard, your speedometer will measure your speed. How fast are you planning to drive? *'Well,'* you might reply. *'I just want to get there as soon as possible, obviously.'* And, sure, if you put your foot down you could get there fast – at least, part of you would be at your destination. The rest of you would still be on its way energetically.

An example of this might be when people jump from one relationship to another, without giving themselves time to breathe, heal and reset their mindset and self-worth. They may look as if they're with a new partner, with a new face, new voice in a new place, but they won't be… and what is likely is that they'll simply attract the same old person with the same old patterns as they did in your near past. If just one part of you races ahead of the rest of you, you'll be forced to retrace your steps if you want to change your patterns.

Sometimes we just wanna be happy and we want to be happy Now! We speed off in search of what happiness could now look like. We are clear about what we don't want but maybe not as clear about what we *do* want. So, we search outside by ourselves, maybe with a new health regime, a different focus. Maybe we might even move from one side of the country to the other. However, the annoying thing about geography is that a relocation only works if you've changed states within yourself.

Instead of being a rally driver on this new section of road ahead, consider slowing down enough to enjoy the scenery/ Remind yourself that you have all the time you need, because you're always in the right place at the right time. Giving yourself a generous amount of space following big events, epiphanies, breakups and emotional upheaval is the kindest gift you can ever give yourself.

Time to be in your own space can rebuild you… if you use the time well and bravely. Even though it may be uncomfortable to experience, standing still and staying in the present moment, can be the best tonic your soul requires. Only in this way will you begin to discern the difference between being lonely and being alone.

1. Respect the rules of divine timing

It is easy to act like a toddler, even when we think we're all grown up. Usually it's to do with time – timeframes, impulses and desires. We're so used to having instant gratification in this high-tech world, we think that everything can find its way to us rapidly. However, as everything is about energy, this is not the case – because when you are impatient, your ego has become involved. Now it's not just between you and the vibes. You've unwittingly created tension and added it to the mix of manifestation.

As much as you may grit your teeth about it, it's important to respect the natural ebb and flow of energy. When you send out a wish, it'll float out beyond you into what Quantum physicists describe as 'the zero-point field' – a spacious area of neutral energy that surrounds you. If you send out a strong wish, it'll ripple the waves and assist in the attraction of your goal. However, if you attempt to change this recipe by adding toddler impatience, you'll ruin the cosmic order.

2. Stop being in such a hurry

If you have a fortunate life, you have already established the basics of food water and shelter. Now you're living with more choice, more options and this is where impatience begins to really take root. If you're feeling impatient, you're holding tension. Tension messes with the Flow.

Synchronicity is never in a hurry. Perfect timing flows according to a sense of energetic eternity, where there are no clocks, schedules, traffic lights and other man-made ways to keep a certain level of tension in the body. If you feel yourself rushing ahead, your vibes will quickly inform you that you've moved out of sync with the Universe. Those traffic lights will turn to red just as you approach, that parking spot will be snapped up just as you see it, you'll miss out on the job vacancy that closed today. Your job is to trust. Your Soul is never in a hurry.

3. Be *clear about your destination*

You've never gotten into your car and wondered where you were going. You knew long before you grabbed your keys and closed the door behind you. Your ultimate challenge is to realise that even though your hands are on the steering wheel, your higher self and your guides are driving. All they require from you is a clear vision, an idea of where you want to go. Just like any taxi-driver in any city of the world.

The clearer you are about how you want to feel in the future, more powerful choices will open to you along the way. Your drivers are not so interested in the house, the boat or the country you crave – what they *really* want to know is how you'd feel once you achieve your desire. For instance, you may feel enormous relief knowing that you have more than enough money to not only pay all of your bills, but easily enjoy the benefits of spontaneous holidays. You might feel immense safety, being wrapped in the arms of a steadfast partner who loves you purely for who you are, rather than what you do. Focus on which feelings you want to go towards.

4. *Enjoy the view with patience and trust*

Now, settle back in the seat and admire the scenery. The only way to do this, is to release the tension that arises from all that habitual overthinking, impatience and fears of the future. A wonderful affirmation to say to yourself as often as you need to, is *'I am always in the right place at the right time.'* As you say those words out loud, you feel your entire body relaxing, your mind soothed.

There's no future, no past, only now – and if you miss the Now, you'll miss the moment. In this moment is the opportunity to relax your entire body, enjoy the colours of the trees and the birds, the comfort of the seat – and most of all, a calm, abiding sense of gratitude that you are still here, in spite of everything.

Chapter 8
stick to the road

It's super easy to set off to your chosen destination, only to be distracted by plenty of fascinating signposts luring you off-track. These represent sudden doubts about your worth, dating someone who's not qualified to be in a relationship, choosing a job that doesn't make you happy (but the money is great!) or being tied to an obligation that your heart isn't involved in.

The purpose of your journey is to find your Purpose. The tricky bit is that you can't find it until you find yourself – free of all those old labels and descriptions you grew up with that battered your self-esteem.

To find out who you are, you'll automatically immerse yourself in all sorts of situations and challenges. Usually, our Souls like to start off in life living in families and environments that are the opposite to who we are. This really helps us clarify what we want.

For instance, I grew up with adult women who were not cuddly and affectionate. I craved warmth, as we will all do, in order to develop a healthy self-esteem. I may have felt lost during childhood and adolescence, but I knew who I wanted to be when I grew up – and that was to be a woman who exuded warmth and whose heart was strong enough to be silly, yet soft enough to see the light.

So, I had to go out and learn how to shed the hard edges of my heart and become the mother I always wanted to have. It took me years... but I got there, only to discover that warmth formed an essential part of my purpose.

Once you become clearer about what you want, the next step is building up the courage to be different. 'Different' just means that you haven't found your people yet. You'll need to close a few doors and go in search of your tribe, your community of humans who recognise you immediately as your frequency is familiar to them.

If you're about to turn off the road at a detour, trust your intuition. It may be one you've been down before. Or it may be one that gets you back on your chosen path even more firmly. Just don't stay off-track too long.

1. You're here to break cycles

Sometimes we travel the same road as our parents and guardians. Generations of your family may have dug and tarred the road that your car is on. If you're not sure, pull over to the side of the road. Take a good, long look. If something doesn't feel quite right... or if it feels that you're travelling this way to gain the approval of others, then it's not your road.

It feels safe and easy to follow what's gone before, right? You won't have to think for yourself, and you won't need to trust that sixth sense of yours. You'll have plenty of rules in your head, with at least one family member assuring you that, *"it's always been this way."* If you're a cycle breaker in your family, you will feel pressure. It'll be scary to fight for your authenticity. You'll be breaking the laws of your clan. And when you do, they'll will do everything they can to pull you back. It's just how things are. If you feel an inner persistent call, a compulsion to go where you need to go, in spite of disapproval, allow yourself to get to the point of 'enough', then you'll possess the power to do it.

2. Resist the irresistibility of temptation

Oh look! Here comes another signpost that says, 'scenic route'. It's a sunny day, you're not in any particular hurry… so perhaps you might consider turning the steering wheel. That's exactly what distraction can be, a seductive invitation to have you forget where you are going.

In Greek mythology, Odysseus was a man who travelled the world for 10 years. His destination was his purpose, to reassert his right to rule Ithaca, an island in Greece. This man encountered a lot of detours on his journey across the seas. He had to pass metaphysical tests, discover his powers, fight monsters, learn how to trust his intuition over external advice and untangle himself from manipulative people. To stop himself and his crew from being distracted from the Sirens, alluring and beautiful mermaid-like creatures urging them to dive overboard and drown, he gave orders to tie themselves to the ship's mast.

Keep your eyes on the road. Ignore gossip. Don't react to the hook of drama or slander. They're all just Sirens, testing your powers.

3. Accept that you are distractable

Whatever you accept, you can change, or you can let go. One of the easiest ways to stop yourself from being distracted, is to accept that you could be. There's no point denying it or trying to pretend you can't. Look at your phone, for example. How hard would it be for you to not look at it for 5, 10, 24 hours? Very!

Once you accept that distractions will always be out there for you, your inner strength steps in and your head gets stubbornly clear. The word is *'resolute'*. This is how we make our own rules – whether it's to be loyal or to cheat in a relationship, to defraud or be honest in our careers, to speak up or stay invisible. Remember you own the power of choice. Acknowledge those dark, light and grey options. Once done, you will be an even more focused driver and a dilemma will soon be in your rear view mirror.

4. Decide whether your destination is the most important

As we grow, we discover that we've had a huge amount of experience in the *'don't want'* basket. We don't want a partner who plays video games all night, because we don't enjoy feeling invisible. We don't want to date someone with a bad temper because we hate walking on eggshells. We'd rather work for a happy leader than a grouchy manager.

It's all about priorities. Once you decide what is the most important priority for you – whether it's to feel good about yourself, perform an amazing service or to feel energised from your work, you can clearly plot the coordinates for your travel towards your goal. Priorities need a lot of energy, a lot of love and focus – a bit like a plant in your apartment that you want to thrive and grow. Synchronicity loves a human who is completely all in.

Chapter 9
do you feel lucky?

Is 'luck' really a thing or is it just excellent energetic timing? Are some people luckier than others? Luck is really being in the right place at the right time. It's a combination of intuition, telepathy and trusting ourselves to act in a moment that feels 'right', rather than let our minds get in the way and have us procrastinate a sudden idea.

The definition of 'coincidence' is 'a remarkable concurrence of events or circumstances without apparent connection'. Synchronicity is when things happen together at the same time.

Then there's this thing called *déjà vu*, when you find yourself in a scene that you've been before. They're always super cool as you know, and in my experience, they occur a couple of weeks before or after a turning point. I think it's your Higher Self reminding you that life is a 'game' – that your job is to do your best, not worry about the other players and get to the end feeling happy that you achieved a dream.

My advice is to consider yourself lucky. If you relax into that belief, you're naturally synchronised, magnetic and open to opportunities. Energetically, there's a difference between 'wish' and 'will'. One's airy-fairy and a little vague, the other has strength and focus – much like an archer placing an arrow into her bow and pointing it at a specific target.

Join me in this energetic game I play every day. It's called the *Money Miracle* technique, although you can substitute the word 'money', for anything else such as relationship, love or health.

This is how it goes: when you wake up in the morning, you say out loud, *"today, I will receive a miracle having to do with money"*. Then you wait and watch. Miracles can be big or tiny – it could be sudden news about a pay rise or just the fact that where you're going shopping, there's a 50% off sale.

Once you spot a miracle, say out loud *"thank you! Now I will receive another miracle having to do with money!"* Then wait with confident expectation for the next miracle to appear. You can roll this energy all day. Once it becomes a habit, the results can be quite amazing. Give it a go.

1. Get ready to manifest

Before you get into the groove of attracting exactly what you want, actively dispel any scepticism. It's really easy and lazy to be negative and cynical. Whether good things or bad things are happening in your life, energetically you are still in the flow of some invisible Universal plan for your life.

Remember the Law of Attraction. What you put out, will come back. If you want more money but send it out with that tension underlying your desire, you'll receive less then what was available. Choose to access the feelings that a happy millionaire or someone in an incredible loving family or relationship would feel every day… relaxed, settled into a certain groove of calmness and *certain* of receiving.

2. Set the boomerang free

When an Aboriginal hunter spot a kangaroo, they traditionally acknowledge and thank the roo for the food that they're about to receive. Then they'll aim their boomerang – and release them. They expect it to circle back to their waiting hands. They're not standing there, worrying about whether it'll return or not. Their anxiety level isn't shooting sky-high because they think it's just a stick. They're also not telling themselves off for dreaming too unrealistically or thinking that this is a really bad idea. They simply relax, considers dinner tonight and waits.

In order to have a manifestation come to you, be willing to suspend all negative mind chatter and place yourself in an open space, ready to receive with grace and gratitude. If you overthink it, the boomerang will return with further complications. Decide on what you want, make it as detailed as possible and let it go. All your vibes need is self-belief. In fact, you have a boomerang in your hunter's pack right now.

3. Develop a constant state of gratitude

Many of us have clean water, a comfy bed, nearby supermarket, access to technology and at least one person on the planet thinks we're special. It's easy to get complacent. When a study was done of lottery winners, it was found that within 12 months of receiving a huge payout, their level of discontent was the same as it was, prior to their big win.

We all tumble backwards sometimes. We think about the woes and worries in our life far more than the gifts and joys. When a bill arrives for you to pay, instead of feeling the tension in your body that comes from times of poverty and struggle, try wearing a new thought, such as *'this company trusts me to be wealthy enough to pay this bill.'* Terminally ill people tend to have more gratitude than the rest of us. Your mission is to not wait until you're dying. Begin now. You are alive. You're not living in a tent in a refugee camp. The birds are singing. The sun is still shining.

4. You'll see it after you believe it

There is a common phrase out there in the world: *"I'll believe it when I see it,"* usually muttered by pessimistic humans who may not actually believe they deserve something. Magic works in upside-down ways. If you don't set a clear goal or visualise your dream with as much clarity and detail as you can imagine, the chances are you won't receive it in the same way. So, first you have to believe. Believe that not only are you worthy of receiving this gift from the universe, but that you can feel it, sense it and get excited by it, as if it is truly winging its way towards you right now.

It took me a solid year of affirming and living out my deserveability to draw to me a terrific partner who adored me for who I was. Magic needs repetition as well as belief. I wrote down my short priority list, focusing on the top three things I wanted in a healthy relationship. I spoke it out loud under the light of the moon and stars almost every night. When he arrived, he had everything on my priority list. You have the same magic within you.

Chapter 10
manage your gears

Have you ever driven behind a really slow driver when you're in a hurry? Whenever we're flustered and impatient, everything slows down – as if the Universe has a wicked sense of humour. We stub our toe, swear, make mistakes, cut corners and shift our gears from fourth to third in an effort to race past the offending driver (who's probably feeling a lot more grateful about life, than we are in that moment).

Everyone's doing it tough right now. Everyone's stressed. Everyone's just hoping life gets a whole lot easier so that they can go back to being happy again. However, our weakness is when we react to outside events with the speed of a racing driver, lightning-quick and usually negative, at times aggressive.

We are energetically positioned for war. We have our hand on our weapon, ready to defend, ready to push, ready to be right.

Your job is to discipline your emotions, and by that, I mean manage them. If you don't learn how to handle your intensity and redirect it into something powerful, like passion instead of rage, you'll remain enslaved by your outside environment.

Now that you're more self-aware, you properly noticed the tightness in your belly which is happening at the same time as your mind is going into hyperactive negativity. It's a bit like OCD – every human has some form of this condition. We can all obsessively focus on something and compulsively repeat that same thought or action, over and over.

Your anger means you are judging or trying to control. We want people to be just like us, but better, more evolved in some way. Then, they would understand our intention behind our behaviour. They'd be kind in response to our reactivity, pat us on the head gently and in the case of a slow driver – speed up obligingly.

Life is not working you up into a frenzy. You are doing it yourself.

1. Live in the middle zone

Managing your emotions does not mean you shut down. What you repress will inevitably explode, and usually in the wrong moment. Everyone's rude sometimes. Some of us are polite to strangers, yet rude and mean to those we love… while the opposite is true for others. It's a question of who we feel safe enough to shout at. Your second choice is to stifle your emotions, which will depress you, because you're beating up yourself.

The solution is to acknowledge how you're feeling, take some breaths, roar like a lion in your car and book a boxing class. If you feel sad, make time to cry. If you feel mad, make time to punch a cushion loudly. Regulate your feelings by giving them a safe method to be expressed. Then you won't need to go around like a grouchy human and blame everybody else.

2. There are no good days and bad days

Sometimes, we keep ourselves safe by deciding to only feel the emotions that we happen to like or are familiar with. For some people, it's grief, for others it's positivity. For example, I have met clients who tell me that they never get angry. What their energy often tells me is that their anger is just disguised under another name. It's still there lurking. Self-acceptance frees us to love ourselves more fully, it heals our inner child, it boosts our self-respect, and it allows all of our emotions to be recognised and accepted.

You don't really have good days and bad days… you have good moments and bad moments. If you can accept that both are unavoidable, and that you will experience, like every other human being on the planet, a smorgasbord of uncomfortable feelings and easy feelings – and let them all be present in your day, you will be mastering a powerful balance of energy within you.

3. Have your own space but not too much

Extroverts need other people around them to charge their energy. Then there are those who need a little bit of mingling and a little bit of quiet time. As an introvert with an extrovert purpose, I need solitude in order to recharge my batteries. I've become very good at giving myself space. One of my delights is not having to talk to anyone for a few days. However, I notice that if I have too much hermit-time, my sensitivity increases around other people. If you find you're veering towards one extreme or the other, try the middle path for a while.

Balance is key. One thing we're not very good at, is measuring time. We work long, arduous hours or maintain a mood longer than it needs to be there. It's exhausting to stay in the same activity, space or vibration for too long. By learning to work in short bursts of energy and then to relax is how you maintain an upbeat, manifesting the Mojo vibe.

4. Judging others by their intentions

Your commitment to self-love is maintaining powerful boundaries around behaviour you judge as unsafe, such as a violence or abuse. In this case, your judgement of the situation is absolutely crucial. With these exceptions, we tend to judge others by their behaviour and ourselves by our intentions. This means we are continually letting ourselves off the hook and slowing down our development. On other days we like to switch it up by shaming and guilting ourselves about our own actions, while idealising other people's seeming perfection.

Observe how quickly you judge yourself and others – then decide to drop this habit, by replacing it with neutral observation. Everyone is good, imperfect, deeply self-conscious and a little insane. Beneath the behaviour of someone you're judging, you'll most likely find fear, shame and a lack of self-love. Just like the money miracle technique, it helps to look for the light in someone. Focus on that, instead of all their imperfections. It's healthier for your spirit.

Chapter 11
how will you know when you get there?

Many years ago, I was serving dinner to my four children when a good friend and neighbour burst in through the door, agitated.

"When do you know it's time?" she asked, almost as if she was talking to herself. Then she looked at me with the pleading look on her face. "How do you know when it's time, time to leave?" I knew she was talking about her unhappy marriage… her constant waiting for his availability, evolution, self-leadership and loving presence.

I could only shake my head in sympathy. We might be able to see when people stay too long in lousy situations, and if asked for our advice, we might willingly give it. However, we will never fully understand the extent of somebody else's lessons. We won't understand the plan they have devised for themselves, their roadmap or their destination. We can offer support, learn from somebody else's bravery, but we must keep driving along our own road.

Look to your own chapters. When we realise a lesson or a chapter is reaching its end, we are becoming conscious. We are no longer on automatic pilot, hoping things will get better. Perhaps we've already learned the lesson contained within that job or that relationship, usually to do with boundaries and self-worth.

Consciousness is the destination of every lesson. It doesn't happen in the brain; it happens in the heart. We come to learn what ancient tribal shamans and wise sages have always known; that it's essential that we live through the heart rather than through the ego.

Consciousness is being acutely aware that you are connected to everything and everyone. It's about feeling the pain of others but learning how to protect your energy from it. It's about understanding that you can choose to love anyone at any time whilst applying wise discernment.

When you feel the clock is ticking, when you hear that 'enough' reverberate around your being, when you become aware that you can be happier elsewhere – then it's time. The rest is honesty and courage. The reward is immense relief and a sense of scary but exciting free-dom, full of strange new possibilities.

1. Consult a wise friend

We all need calm counsel in the middle of the storm.
We all need a fresh eye on our skewed, tight perspective. Sometimes all we need for clarity, is the company
of someone that we perceive is healthier in some way.
Sometimes it's a single sentence of wisdom we hear,
that hits us squarely in the centre of our forehead –
a clear sudden understanding that we need to head
towards that door before it slams shut for another long
cycle.

If you want to stay in your pattern, you'll have friends
who are in a similar situation, but choosing to stay in
place. Their desensitisation towards the trauma of their
everyday experiences, will make you feel that yours isn't
so bad after all. Once you start to minimise the impact
of your experiences, you'll stay stuck. Find a functional
friend who is trustworthy enough to hear you or call
your local free counselling line and talk anonymously
to a kind stranger on the other end of the phone. This
is what self-love looks like in a time of great difficulty.
The ability to reach out is courageous, necessary and
it'll stop you from becoming invisible inside your own
pain.

2. Recognise what you've learned

Be grateful to the worst of teachers that you've had to put up with in your life. They're the ones who teach us the most, the unloving ones, the harsh ones, the ones that put us through hell and back. Be grateful for the tough times, for you'll appreciate the good times so much more. Recognise your progress and keep growing.

Once upon a time, after a boyfriend broke up with me, I asked for his feedback on what made me so difficult to be with. For the first month, I took care of my emotions, clearing my grief and anger in inner child ways and accompanied by blankets, tissues and treats. Then I drove over to his house with my notepad and interviewed him briefly. He was helpful. It was useful. I didn't shame myself. Instead, I worked on my character flaws so that I could become the partner I wanted. And it worked!

3. Check if the lesson has passed its expiry date

The fastest way to know whether you might be staying in a lesson long after it should've ended, is to notice how many times the pattern goes around and around. If you're having the same argument repeatedly, if you are feeling drained and exhausted rather than energised and joyous, you're still spinning in circles and will only get increasingly ungrounded and dizzy.

Expiry dates on situations and relationships are exactly the same as that jar of tomato paste that's been sitting in your fridge door for two years. You always planned to use it for that wonderful dinner party once your life was back on an even keel or when you could pretend that everything was okay. But if you open the jar, you'll notice all the penicillin that is growing in there. That's the real message from the Universe. Take the medicine. Learn what you came to learn about yourself. Then get the hell out.

4. Make sure you're a human being, not a zombie

If you've ever lingered for too long in a relationship
with a narcissist or a bully, you'll turn into a zombie.
To survive the gaslighting, abusive words and actions,
you'll shut down, which will in turn block your intuition, shut out your guides and your self-worth will be
replaced by even more shame and doubt to immobilise
you further.

Living as a shell of a human being who pretends not to
care about the eggshells under your feet destroys your
Mojo. With each day you excuse increasingly terrible
behaviour, your light grows dimmer. You wait for the
event that will have it end and you fervently hope it
won't be by your death. That's how bad it gets. Trust
me, I've been there. It took all my strength to change
my situation, but I did it, because I stuck to my one
rule: 'if it looks like it's going to happen a second time
then it's over.' It's always time to leave an abusive relationship.

Chapter 12
you got this

Okay, so I'm thinking you're a pretty good driver so far.

You've picked up this book for a start... and it feels to me that you ready to progress your life. You have a dream, a vision that you may have begun as a child that you want to inch even closer towards now. You've come to understand that one of the main lessons in this entire life was for you to realise that you're the adult with free choice now.

You've stopped comparing yourself to other people. You now emulate the ones you admire greatly for their courage and growth.

You've started balancing your self-esteem by understanding that everybody is equal, each with their own shadow and light, smarts and stoopidness.

That old emotional wound you used to keep picking at, is beginning to heal because you really want to get on with life and enjoy yourself.

You're loving yourself more than you ever have. You're beginning to receive compliments with more grace, with a simple 'thank you', rather than batting them away quickly or returning the compliment, like back in the old days when you used to do conditional love.

You've realised that there's something about you that other people really like. These days, you're much more aware of your attributes, wittiness, cute quirks, skills, talents and general sassiness.

You've taken the best qualities of your parents and guardians, and you've tossed out the rest, by breaking cycles and making your own rules. Nowadays, you view people who are behaving in petulant, mean-spirited or dramatic ways as being stuck in their ignored inner children.

You've put your mind in its place and have started training your mindset to follow your glorious lead towards healing and happiness. It's been trotting along behind you like an obedient puppy, now it knows you're taking care of your inner child and you're a safe place to be.

And you're becoming more authentic every day. It's feeling easier just to be yourself, in any given moment. You're noticing the magic that's happening just because people are finding it easy to connect with you who's not wearing a mask.

You've realised you've nothing to prove to anybody else. You no longer apologise when you've done nothing wrong, nor justify your decisions or defend your choices.

Your boundaries are rock-solid. You understand that mixed signals now mean 'no'. You trust people's vibes and actions more than their promises and excuses. You now leave toxic situations as soon as a red flag appears because you love yourself enough to take good care of you.

You realise that you are incredibly valuable, like a shiny, unscratched jewel – and that if you're not treated with a certain level of respect, then you don't require their presence in your life.

You no longer strive to be perfect, just conscious.

You no longer need to be loved by somebody else because that job is now a full-time passion of yours. You understand the power of magnetism and notice that you are attracting people who are mirroring your self-worth with their own.

You laugh a whole lot more. Deep belly laughs. Now you're much slower to criticise, you have more space for joy.

You're teaching people how to treat you and it's amazing how things have shifted in your life. The old you used to do everything for others in the hope that you'd get the appreciation you craved… but now that you're all full up on your own daily self-appreciation, free to serve others because you've prioritised your own energy and peace first. In fact, you've actually started to give more, effortlessly simply by being yourself.

You're trusting your belly more than your head. Your intuition is becoming muscly and well-toned. You're tuning into people's energy rather than relying on their words and actions.

Above all, you've become grateful for the little things in life and the big things in life. You live more in the moment now and consequently feel calmer. What surprises you is how increasingly easy it is to just *be*.

When you look back at your life, when you look back at the road that you've been driving on all this time, with all of its crazy detours, potholes and ditches , you've begun to realise how important all those challenges were, for your spirit to become resilient, your heart braver and your inner wisdom to be birthed into light.

You got this. *I can feel it.*

Lucy Baker
is the Mother of <u>The Lucy Daily</u>
and the author of four other books,
available through Amazon or her website:

<u>The Yoga of Relationship</u> (inner child healing)

<u>Past Lives, Present Baggage</u> (the impact of past lives)

<u>It's Not Anxiety, It's Urgency</u> (a more in-depth guide to Life)

<u>Get The Hex Away From Me</u> (energetic protection)

Lucy works as a wisdom-keeper,
recognised as shaman by the indigenous in the mid-90s
and teaches online and face to face workshops,
classes and retreats from her homebase in Australia.
She also sees many clients for personal sessions,
usually humans who are at turning points.

For more information, visit lucybaker.net

Please email me if you are on your road of recovery, power and general sassiness and let me know how it's going!

In the meantime, be forearmed by reading *The Lucy Daily*, posted every day via Facebook and Instagram.

Share it with those in need of a hug each morning, with my gratitude.

As Ram Dass said,

"we're all just walking each other Home."

You still got this. x